The poems in *The Book of the Floating World* are poems of increasing complexity. That is to say, for me, reading the book twice, three times, ten times, has layered its subject(s) further and further behind the sighting of the opaque lens, while simultaneously bringing more layers to the surface.

— Brandon Shamoda *Word For/Word: A Journal of New Writing* #8

The lyrics in this book reward slow and thoughtful rereadings. The photography and poetry are haunting.

—Marcus Slease, *Octopus Magazine* #4

In *The Book of the Floating World*, the poet imagines his way into the past, constructing his dead father's experience of occupation Japan, and at the same time reflecting eloquently on the fallibility of such an endeavor. With his only evidence a group of photographs taken by his father, Thompson moves beyond those particular images to summon up vivid fragments of scenes cradled in the narrator's subtle, intelligent consciousness. The poems are elegant, elegiac meditations on the nature of personal history and mortality. In the book as a whole, the continuous and arresting conjunctions of past and present give *The Book of the Floating World* a quality of timelessness.

—Angela Davis-Gardner, author of *Felice* and *Forms of Shelter*

Part moral memoir, part imagined life of the father, part imagined history, part solid history, this unusual combination of verbal and visual—of the then seen from the perspective of now—makes a rare and interesting book.

—Betty Adcock, author of *The Difficult Wheel* and *Intervale*

The Book of the Floating World

Also by Jon Thompson

Fiction, Crime and Empire

The Book of the Floating World

Jon Thompson

Parlor Press
West Lafayette, Indiana
www.parlorpress.com

The photographs in *The Book of the Floating World* were taken by sculptor
William J. Thompson.

Parlor Press LLC, West Lafayette, Indiana 47906

Printed in the United States of America
S A N: 2 5 4 - 8 8 7 9
Library of Congress Cataloging in Publication Data

Thompson, Jon, 1959-
  The book of the floating world / Jon Thompson.
      p. cm.
  Poems.
  Includes index.
  ISBN-13: 978-1-60235-013-7 (pbk. : alk. paper)
  I. Title.
  PS3620.H6833B66 2007
  811'.6--dc22

                                         2007024844

Printed on acid-free paper.
Cover illustration: "Black Market" by William J. Thompson
Cover design by David Blakesley

Parlor Press, LLC is an independent publisher of scholarly and trade titles in print and multimedia
formats. Versions of this book are available in cloth and electronic formats from Parlor Press on the
WWW at http://www.parlorpress.com and at online and brick-and-mortar bookstores everywhere.
For submission information or to find out about Parlor Press publications, write to Parlor Press, 816
Robinson St., West Lafayette, Indiana, 47906, or e-mail editor@parlorpress.com.

For my father,
William J. Thompson

Time goes from present to past.

—Dogen

Contents

Acknowledgments

Grateful acknowledgment is made to the following journals in whose pages some of these poems first appeared: *Faultline*, *The Iowa Review*, *Potomac Review*, *Prism International*, *Quarterly West*, and *Visions International*.

I owe a special debt of gratitude to Ger Killeen, Angela Davis-Gardner, Nick Halpern, John Balaban, and Betty Adcock for their detailed readings of the manuscript, and to all those who supported this project. Thanks, too, to North Carolina State University for a CHASS Summer Stipend, which provided a grant at a critical time. And thanks, too, to David Blakesley, who helped make this book possible.

The Book of the Floating World

I

Good and evil we know in the field of this world grow up almost inseparably.

—John Milton, *Areopagitica*

Black Market

Tokyo, 1946

In the burned-out open-air square
        there are no stalls animals cars or banners
only thousands of men some still in uniform some in partial uniforms
        some in topcoats and fedoras some in Chinese coats looking
for something that can't be found
        the disaster evident in the piles of valuables spread on blankets
the man-clusters drift slowly
        into new clusters
everyone is looking down
        the catastrophe has already
happened this is the post-apocalypse all the odd jumble
        of the past the detritus of former lives is struggling
to be reborn in the buying and selling
        from far off a man squats on his haunches
inspecting a book & elsewhere
        a tall man in black is refusing a sale
further back a white-hot light is boiling overhead
        everyone is becoming less and less
they are fading
        not even becoming a negative of themselves
and under that light
        the buildings are dissolving
the unnatural musical light is breaking
        in waves
over a future which is unaware

Absolution

What can we take from the past
    a past that was never anything more than a succession
of marked and unmarked moments
    continuously flowing together or flown
each the ancestor to the other
    so little so much against the weight of darkness
a lifetime ago the winter light offered a kind of absolution
    it drenched the stones of that city with the openness
of summer on one corner a monk and a nun stand by a building chanting
    his head is shaved hers is hooded
they are swathed in long robes
    the woven basket at their feet is full of alms
holding onto short paddle-drums
    they neither regard nor disregard the people passing by
but give witness to those things beyond the eye
    that define the complexion of each day
the vast tissue of connections
    that decides each act
their day nothing less than the open acknowledgment
    of unpayable debts
a practice like fully living or dying
    like seeing or hearing for the first time
like the gift of giving or receiving freely
    like the world suddenly without sound
or suddenly full of it

Thresholds

In front of the temple there's a large bronze gong
    and a long thick rope
the officer looking into his viewfinder
    has approached its threshold
as a stranger beholding a strange place without
    God or gods
stopped before its dim interior he wants
    to capture its foreignness for the future
for now he is still before the folding doors of the entrance
    he is looking in
to take away the image of the tall brass incense tree
    the story of ascending smoke which is his story
a story in which he does not exist
    a story in which the photographer of the photographer does not exist
a story in which the I that writes these lines
    does not exist
a story in which the photo fades with the smoking tree
    a story in which the story gets in the way
of the story that cannot be told

Traffic

Who will remember this long Edwardian boulevard
    with electric trams running up and down it
like Vienna fin-de-siècle except
    the thoroughfares have been cleared
only American jeeps scoot along them
    the people jam the cordoned-off sidewalks where there
is no space the boulevard by contrast is all space
    as if cleared for a parade in the air hangs
a sharp sense of anticipation
    an openness beyond the ordinary a strangeness
from the burnt-out smoke-damaged buildings
    standing shoulder-to-shoulder
with the untouched ones & no one looks twice
    in the hustle and bustle men and women thread the crowded sidewalks
eyes fixed on the next thing to do
    and as if by agreement neither side pays any mind to the other
jeeps hurtle through the opened spaces &
    pedestrians disembark from trams warming from the sunlight
of an ordinary spring day
    & close by an ambulance waits in the shadow of the stopped tram
and the uniformed policeman who directs the traffic
    looks from a distance like a toy soldier
his right arm stiffly extended to indicate
    a right of way or a formal salute
to the undirected streams which flow in front of him
    behind him to his left to his right

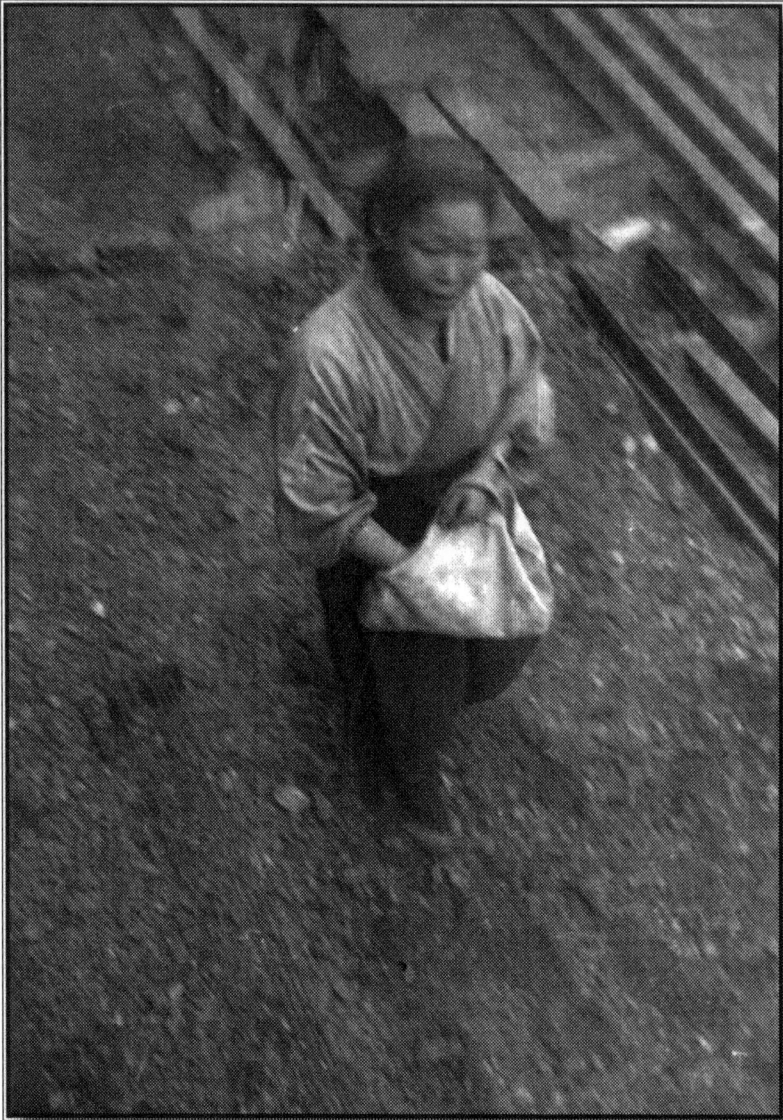

Writing History

If everything becomes everything else
    if every event touches every other event
creates it reverberates through and beyond it
    then nothing is inconsequential and history
is both what we are and what we are becoming
    a continuous making and unmaking a story of unspeakable
intimacy and unspeakable loss here is a photograph
    of winter and dusk and train tracks
and a grimy factory woman who is trying to make her way home
    someone who has passed out of one history
into another where the blanks are unfillable
    we know so little but on that
we base everything
    & the photographer who is about to take her photograph
he does not know her
    does not know her reasons his own this man who became
the photograph I now hold in my hand how
    the blanks & spaces fill the years
how much the body the tired body
    the photographed body the figurative body
depends upon them
    the spaces that loom larger longer wider
what was it you saw when you glanced up at him
    that man who lived in a world which still thought
the world was all in the things you could see

On Permanence

There's a space between now and then
     an in-betweenness which is indwelling
in the flat-seeming earth and round-seeming sky
     an indwelling in the indistinctness between them
is there really a Japanese sky a New England sky
     a northern sky a southern sky
when you look up at it during the brilliance of day or during the brilliance of night
     it is only *it* foreign and familiar
and there is only a sense of traveling
     with the pang of something suddenly remembered
or suddenly forgotten
     of living with the awareness
of being between stage left and stage right
     only the stage is never there
or is only a stage for the idea of a stage
     what is there to hold onto
as soon as you think of it it is gone
     the players have vanished
you have vanished
     how can it be that the stones are the same
the trees are the same the earth is the same

Imperial Palace

A deep moat a bridge & a high white castle
stock still in a stand of trees
in its distance & detachment it is perfection
achieved even the painted-in sky has
a beauty equal to divinity and on
any day of the week there is death
in the glassy water death in the arch
of the bridge death in the precision
of the unmortared walls death
in the emptiness between words

Idolatry

From the impassive heights
    of history
Kusunoki reigns in his nostril-flaring mount
    he is alive he is dead
the mail headdress of his war-helmet is
    unyielding before the wind
that carries the stench of defeat
    before that
death is a duty
    what of the will that would
bend everything to it
    vanquish the legions of weakness within
& become through that
    a force that cannot be turned back
a movement of pure will driving through
    the legions of the dead who live with defeat
& build & build again in the rubble of each new day
    what stones will honor them
what monuments to the survivors of heroes

The Names

Tokyo, G.H.Q.

In that city of cherry blossoms and wide avenues
        the dimensions loom larger
larger than the names we have for them
        how do you build a new nation
how do you forget the old one
        what it did what was done to it in the name of
names walls of flames sent up their singing
        in the name of names cities became
their shadows
        from far off you could hear the wind sighing over long grass
the smallest sounds as it raised sun-filled sheers
        that morning must have been warm and bright
tinged with the tang of promise
        in the glassy pool in front
Roman lines shimmer into ripples
        and in the early morning light a pine-tree bough
thickly-clustered with needles
        protrudes into the side of this old old photograph
it is not clear whether it too is reflected
        in the light-spangled water below it is not clear what gets
copied when an image is taken of an image

At Shinjuku Station

In the shadow of a moment
 the labor of uncorruption–
the light-struck American faces disappear
 into islands of bewilderment
a place where letters are an art & emptiness
 a virtue
in the photograph everything is sepia
 and the Japanese woman bearing parcels on the opposite platform
looks at the GIs with interest
 and the boy in the military uniform with the sash and cap
looks on with interest
 and the middle-aged man forging ahead of them looks
back at them with interest
 but no one looks at the billboarded bright-faced woman
& the impossibly bright-faced man
 exhorting everyone to buy their way to happiness
only curiosity
 to see the other
looking life-like so
 real & free

Blossoms

Dark young eyes on
The strangeness of a world passing
In its long slow going
His wide almond eyes so
Rich in unknowing
Even the morning light reverences them
As it shines upon the dream
That on this day at this time
A stranger would come along nothing then is only strange
Not barbarians not death not the light that plays
Across your wide fearless face would that you never felt fear
The tremor in the hands uncontrollable the mind all of a sudden
A foreign land occupied I'm in a dark dark place fear
Not in that land over the sea there is a nation
Of children like the old tree in the children's park
Imperturbable where innocence takes root
Blossoms are not the only flowers

Empire

Someone must be dead the stars
        fly at half mast
over the implacable marble white building
        with wrought-iron balconies
even in the sun it is cold the whiteness withholds itself
        a whiteness of myth and the end of myth
the whiteness of truth and the end of truth
        fronted by a foyer of large Roman pillars
its vastness speaks
        of the new imperium another empire
at its zenith bone-white untouchable impregnable
        after the war everything speaks for itself
after the war red and yellow became very popular she said
        I loved yellows lemon yellows melon yellow mustard yellow
people said yellow
        is the color of lost love I didn't care she said
I liked it

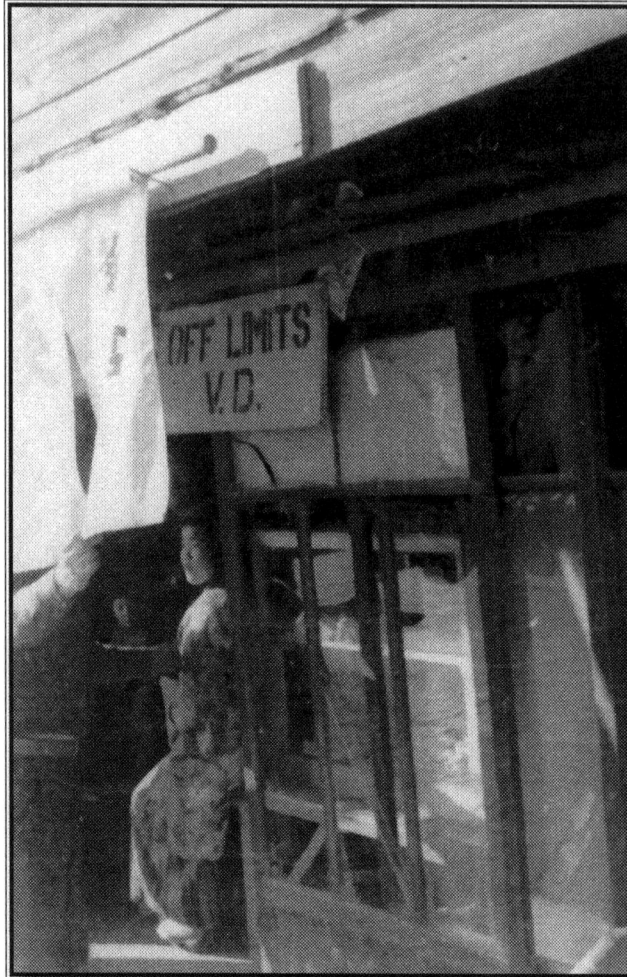

The Drape of Silk

In a flower-rich kimono a motionlessness of disquiet—
    she sits beneath a sign stenciled "OFF LIMITS VD"
the white MP before her is gesturing at something in the distance
    a porcelain depthlessness
is shrouded by the shop's exterior white curtain
    in the photograph light glances off the plate glass shop windows
his finger jabs the sun-soaked air
    everywhere the surfaces of things reflect back
broken images of themselves
    from the doorway a small half-moon face
is half-hidden from the light that flashes off
    her drape of silk & unreasoning goes everywhere

The Cranes

Presentiments of the here and now.
Alien to the god of Abraham,
To blood-sacrifice blood-bond blood-love,
The small altar before the city temple
Is a wonder cabinet
Of nooks & crannies,
Miniature wooden boxes,
Rice cakes and lotus-plays.
Before it no heaven
No sacrifice no death &
The vague light shimmering inside
Backlights the folded paper cranes;
The fragile elegant bodies gleam
In a darkness not there.

Faithfulness

What is faithfulness to whom and to what does it refer
    is being faithful to an old bond
more faithful than being faithful to a new one
    and where does faith come in
if you feel the urge pray pray to Mary
    O Mother of God the urge
what art you made of it
    you for whom faith was angelic
a wavering of light in a white-washed room
    O mother I remember you in that room fading
at the end of the day
    at the end of another an officer is waiting at a station
of thick shadows & narrowed slats of light
    souvenirs bulge out of the duffel bag he's sitting on
arms folded he's ready to return to a world
    in which foreignness has been exiled
a world in which the woman sitting beside him is
    already fading & memory
a matter of what you can trust yourself to be

At the Gate

At the top of a long flight of stone steps
    in front of a thick old grove
stands a tall white Torii gate
    memento to the living and the dead
it rears up like some huge hieroglyph
    beneath a bland unremarkable sky
dreamlike but earthly
    like something prehistoric or archetypal
something created out of mind
    a gateway to the unspoken life of a place
in passing through it there is purification before death
    and a way beyond it
for the dead are material only lost to us
    if we relinquish them for
we live in a world where hatred and desire
    are as durable as stone

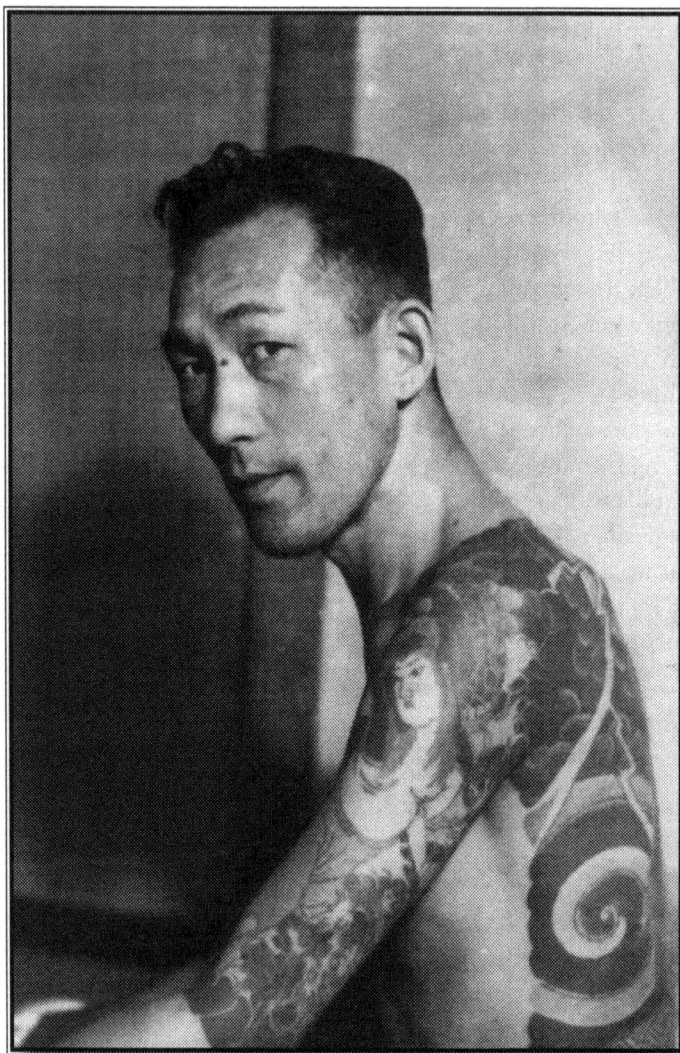

Body/Art

I

When Bodhidarma was asked by the Chinese Emperor Wu
"What is the meaning of the sacred truth?"

Bodhidarma replied "Limitlessly open
Nothing is sacred."

In the yellowed photograph
the tall thin man has disrobed

shedding all pretense of nakedness.
Arms; attention; side.

Centuries of hand-art
bloom on his back his buttocks and thighs.

Still holding the memory
of his body

the long black robe he wore
hangs in front of him.

Across his long slender back
a disciple of Daruma

unscrolls the scriptures
on behalf of a redeemable world.

Limitlessly open
he is the book of his body

sacred & profane
textual & physical

a book of heaven
& a book of hell

in which every
character of every line

inscribed upon his skin
rejoices in

the beauty of heresy
& the worlds to come.

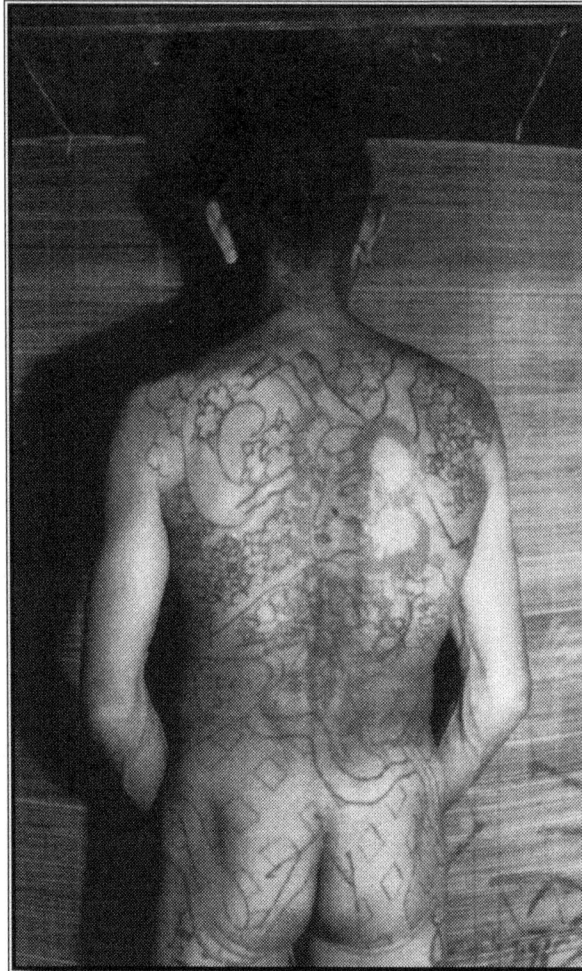

II

From the bony refuge
of the ascetic's back

bristly-headed Oniwaka glares
past you

He who bears the image
bares himself before you.

Lines riot across
his smooth shoulders

his clavicles his narrow hips
buttocks & thighs.

After the incisions
his skin will become

an Edo intaglio of living
scarlets & greens—

a thing to be seen uncovered a beautiful
thing

in the midst of fear.
Soon cherry blossoms will bloom

against the mountains and skies
of his body.

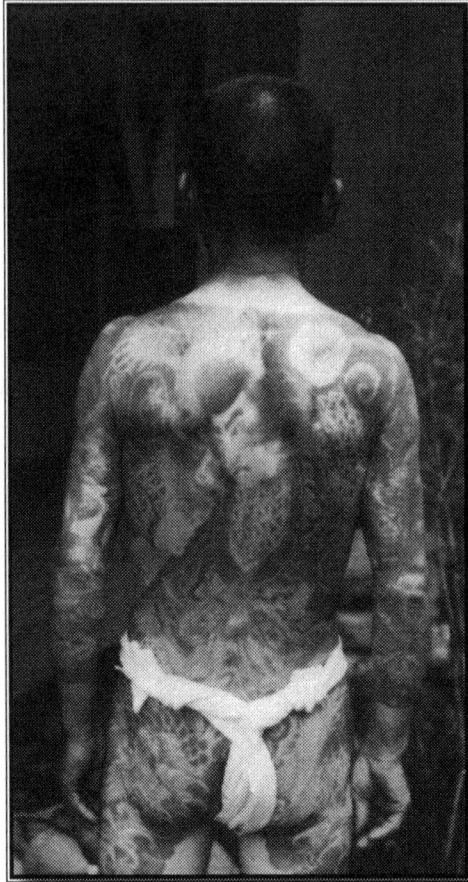

III

1.

Above his white *fundoshi* Kuniyoshi's
magnificent Rochishin from Shih Nai-an's

Suikoden fights
his battles against corruption,

his thick eyebrows knitted in anger
avenging sword in hand,

he is the outlaw out to cleanse
the impure world of its impurities.

2.
The ferret face of the thug
who thus pays him homage

knows much about cleansing.
Foamy waves of pink cherry blossoms

& white chrysanthemums crash & roll
across the skin of ribs, arms & thighs.

In the flotsam and jetsam
of a salty sea-wash

the revolt of the fantastic
triumphs over taboo.

Nakama he is material, maker,
made.

Self-Portrait

How to draw yourself how to shade
       the unseen so that something of you will be seen
how to be on paper so that you can remember
       who you are or what you then thought you were
I never saw you that young
       the blueness of your eyes made
theological by the roundness of the specs
       the long nose & thin high-school face
offset by a tightly-knotted military tie
       & the cigarette dangling off the lips
is the instance of capability
       with the look of irony in
the faintly drawn lines in the eyes
       which look away
avoiding your gaze & mine
       how to read the darkness
blossoming at the nape of your neck
       how your smooth young face
ignores it
       & bending forward
wills its own satisfaction

Of Beauty

And what of beauty
    its monumentality & presence
its unexpected gracefulness & grand
    illusions take for instance the imperial palace
which rises up on high stone walls its many levels of
    tiled triangular houses ascend
to the eye of heaven
    it speaks the old hieratic language
of royalty warriors & castes
    out of fear it creates it
& its fastidious hierarchies impose themselves
    upon the curious as an awe which countenances
no challenge this then is beauty & the absolute
    emptiness around it makes it so

Honganji Temple

Tsukiji, Tokyo

In the darkness there is a white veil
     a bride and a groom
kneeling at the front of the temple watching
     a robed priest perform the rites of union
they are watching him bowing to something unseen
     at a side altar which is also unseen
in this temple it is enough to recite only once
     with absolute faith and sincerity the name of Amida
in order to be saved
     there is so much darkness
and so much faith the flecks of light fall flash
     & fade in witness to them both
in the darkness all attention is on the unseen drama
     transpiring before them
the breath going in coming out
     the pattern the rhythm is louder than words
no one knows what is being witnessed
     no one knows
the places faith will take them to

Honganji Temple II

Let us not have words
    that stand for things let us not have things
that stand for other things let us not
    let this nave stand for love or loss
or departure let everything be as it was
    whenever that was let the room be
as it was huge drafty and dim
    yet full of the scent of incense and ceremony
let everything stand for itself be for itself
    and the room and everything in it
will not be the world will not be the memory of desire
    will not be the cry of desire
or just the cry echoing in the space of desire
    whatever it was it had something to do with
the echoes of words something to do with
    the silence after them
and who they were

II

Here hurry and delay have no bearing;
an instant is ten thousand years.
"Here" and "not here" don't apply either.
Everywhere is right before your eyes.
The tiny is the same as the large
once boundaries are forgotten;
the huge is the same as the small...

—Seng Ts'an

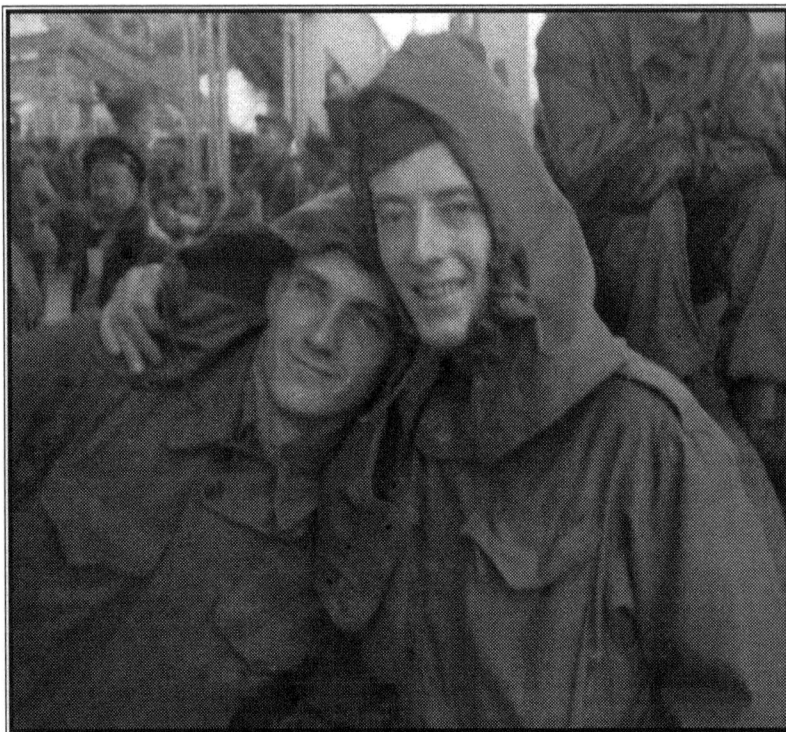

1945

Barely day & overcast everyone on board is on deck men everywhere are
milling about it must be cold everyone is wearing coats and gloves the camera
zeroes in on two friends their heavy hoods monastic
they are young & all-American as they lean together for their picture
one looks at the camera and rests his head on his friend's shoulder the other has his
arm draped about him protectively in tenderness they are handsome &
clear-eyed & dreamy look their clean-shaven faces say we have our whole lives
ahead of us this is a mere jaunt an adventure how can it be they are gone

Under Water

Like some half-lived resurrection
     in which wave after wave seeks shore
sinks and elsewhere reappears
     a flat black surf ripples out and back
& the land rising out of it is little more than
     a line on the horizon a foggy grey mass
an afterthought over which pewter light and salt spray play
     & being distant it can be anything
a tale of tiered temples and cloistered beauty
     or the very brush-stroke of cruelty
anything or nothing at all a chimera within a chimera
     what would you say is there a road to go back to
that place to the ruins that have made us
     is there anyone who would want to go down it
say say something of that place
     say something of the land that slips under lapping water
say something of what it was that made you me

Asaka

How to measure the distance from there to here
The sepia-tinted village with
The shanty-town main-street small shops
& feudal poverty
The peacefulness of a cyclist riding toward you
The past tolling like a bronze bell in the breeze

Working

The steep thatched roof of the farmhouse in the distance overlooks
    long rows of rice seedlings in which are buried
old sadnesses
    so much work day after day to make that marriage of sun and soil work
under a changing sky the story is unchanging
    row after row hugs the land like
a memory of the past you cannot now know
    now is never when you say it is
it is always a memory now it is silent now the wind rises
    it swells full of the silvery sounds of rain in darkness &
the clean rush of rain when night sweeps in
    now you take my hand in yours & open it
now my palms are pressing yours pressing the angry red flesh
    that will not relinquish its rage
now it is night now you are up pacing a world away
    now you are the son of fears that have taken up arms & will not be beaten
their red-eyed dead haunt me what is it
    why is it the fox thou hast found me out
why this wilderness now I am forsaken
    a leper to what I was
now mind is a memory
    body is a memory now here I am the wind the dark wind is rising
now you are among the fallen
    their slender stone urns have gone soft with age and moss
and the slender arms of their stone lovers stretch out
    to one another now there is still time
working the farmer bends over the rows in his field
    working

A New Sky

In the foreground and in the background and in the distance
    platoons of helmets are marching up a paved road
the sunlight is bright on the shoulders
    as they march over cracks
slender shadows crisscross the blackness of their boots
    the uniformed men march not in rigid formation
but loosely relaxed without weapons
    soon they will come across more shadows
& the patient starkness of more trees
    they march as if there were no need for violence weaponry or war
under a new sky
    a sky without sky a blinding whiteness
where clouds once were
    a skyless sky
under which appearance is more than force
    likeness more than difference
brightness more than sun

Origin of Disaster

It's a fragment from the imagination of disaster
    the bombed-out barracks in the army base
surrounded by rubble
    speaks the language of order
the anarchy it has at its heart
    the secret need
it has to undo all that spit and polish
    to brilliantly take the world apart
to make the tidiness of towns
    & cities & roads disappear
to make horns and houses and horses fly up
    into air takes
imagination
    "when I say jump I want you to say how high"
we can only hate what we know
    how much loyalty is rooted in the desire
to defend that which we can't bear to hate

Double Exposure

In the aftermath nothing is impossible
    nothing unthinkable
when the imagination redefines the borders
    the countries cannot be found on maps
and people live between what they were
    and what they imagine themselves to be
or between what they are
    and what they are imagined to be
the high-school student wearing a Japanese army cap
    and a cast-off white technician's coat
is busy rummaging through the Signal Corp's trash-filled oil drums
    when he turns to find himself remade
in a book in which he will always be a scavenger
    here his eyes can never smolder and they don't
as they flicker over the face of the foreigner
    who half-immortalizes him
he knows he is just in time to witness the art
    by which he becomes the eater of trash
the user of refuse one of the lucky ones
    and his only response is the leaden impassivity of his face
this accident he knows
    but he is unaware of the accident of double exposure
whereby suddenly he is standing in a radiant field
    that stretches for days
to reach some steeply-wooded mountains
    ceremonially-banded by huge swaths of flowing white sheets
rivers of them flowing up and down and across the mountain slopes
    a ritual by which the land is shrouded
for that which cannot be atoned

The Emperor

At the end of the road the sky shows the loss
    of divinity
the things people believed in torn
    the sky is torn in two
on one side
    unimaginable brightness
on the other rain-swollen clouds
    gathered in dark augury
can the two be one
    can the one be one
on one side of the road a battalion of tenderfoots
    is falling out directly opposite
a dusty farmer who with horse and cart
    is guiding his family home
for each that which was divine
    is now gone a curiosity
flame-whitened to ash
    one soldier steps out to take a souvenir shot
a military jeep whips by
    after god dies
innocence is the only idol

The Death of Form

To not misunderstand
        to not be the thing the other
thought you were
        the thing you thought you were
the mother-father-daughter family working
        the roadside stand have faces
wreathed in smiles that float above
        snacks stacked next to the beverage bottles with
the bird-on-the-bough label
        cherry-blossom air flows
through the lattice work behind them
        the exchange open
but not nakedly commercial
        the coin of regard passed
and taken
        in the faith that nothing shall interfere
that the past is past
        everything
is different
        is graciousness less
because it is conventional
        ordered for the occasion
or after the death of form
        is form above all what is needed
how do you go on when
        ignorance is gone
what to do what to say
        when too much has been said
when all form
        belongs to the dead

Wilderness

The emptiness of them is almost American.
A glimpse of the next war when everyone
Will be taken
But the land will be left intact.
The neatly-tilled rows stretch on and on,
Without a whisper of wilderness,
An epitaph to what once was.
There is no one no one but the ghosts
Of those who once tended them.
And the telephone poles standing
In the middle of each field
Are like ancient totems
Over which dead voices hum
Murmuring
Over a bewildered land.

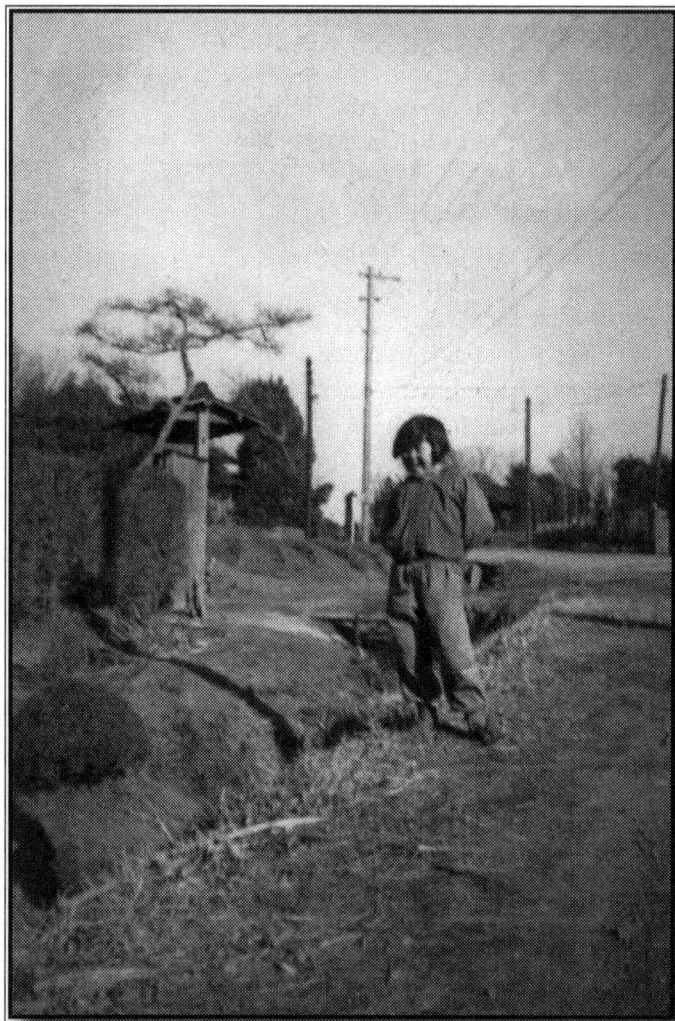

Marginalia

In the mixing of land and sky a featureless landscape—
    the painting of the moment sweeps back
to the enigma of the transitory wherein nothing ever is left behind
    the traces of it scored in the writing
in the writing of the sky & its erasure
    the tyranny of the image making beautiful
the myth of the present
    which empties out all
the pasts leading up to it
    for centuries the flatness of the land has melted
into this rice white sky
    for centuries the girl with the page-boy cut
has stood by the roadside beneath a landscape of her unmaking
    in this book she is ghostly and familiar
a sign above a script of fading signs
    with a face smiling as if she were like
the pine tree behind her
    simple self-evident there

Mount Fuji

Thrusting up out of a blanket of clouds
Black and warrior-like
It is both terrible and heavenly
With its white-crowned cone
Exulting beneath a blacker sky.
No wonder it is
Mythical and real
Forever there and not
Vanishing on the edge of the believable.
No wonder pilgrims ascend it
Laboring up its steep slopes to make offerings
At the shrine of cherry blossoms
Not just to appease but to honor
The hungry ghosts that have fled there
Only to be banished
From the book of black pages.
The mountain the clouds the ravines
Have been sundered in two
Rent from top to bottom .
One hundred and one views of it
And it's no less imaginary than true.

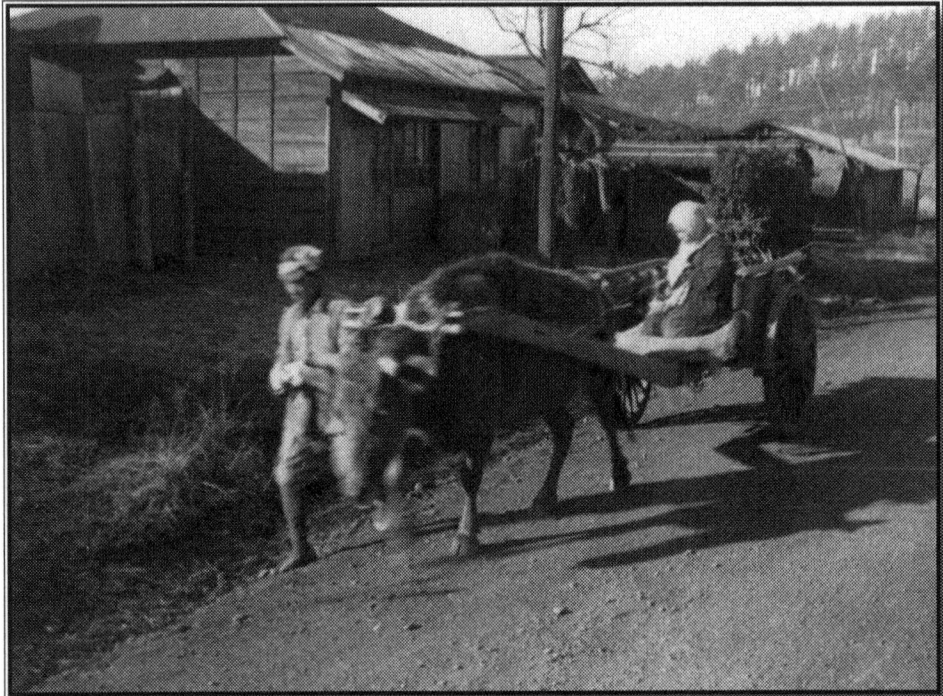

The Ox

Each stone in the road stands out
    each step blurs into a past past knowing
next to the farmer his ox pulls the cart
    on which his wife kneels
how old this story is—
    the worn tunic the threadbare scarf—
in their stillness they've already blurred into
    another century's calm reprise
what is there to do other than that which you do
    day after day a life of work in which war
makes war on ordinary life
    each step made along the road
brings home the choices never had & never made
    the destiny of a nation is written
in the hands

In Play

Unaccountable the blaze of childhood—
    to play all day in the dusty lane
beneath the sloping tiled roof
    and feel nothing but exhilaration
all terror shed
    if the freedom they have
were to be always simply there
    then work would be different
he would be different she would be different
    you would be different the world would be different
would you have approved
    of a world of play
where pleasure was its only end
    its own end
could there be
    an art of play without sacrifice without discipline
without apprenticeship or discipleship
    what would it benefit
if a man gains the world and loses his soul
    what would the world be without it
what would the world be without the knowledge
    that comes from suffering
would we be gaining or losing it

Legacy

Nothing more distant from memory
    nothing more decisive
than the first pain
    to be small in it without language
is to be adrift without a beginning or end
    the toddler in the patched crazy-quilt kimono
is screaming
    the tiny hand held high clutches
the insubstantiality of air her grief-stricken face
    dissolves into white terror
while the mother supports her back
    this ministry the only form
of redemption there is
    & our only glimmering
as to who we might be able to become
    the only clue to the unrecoverable origins
when in woe we were
    never less than the sum of those
whose lives too
    were once held in other people's hands

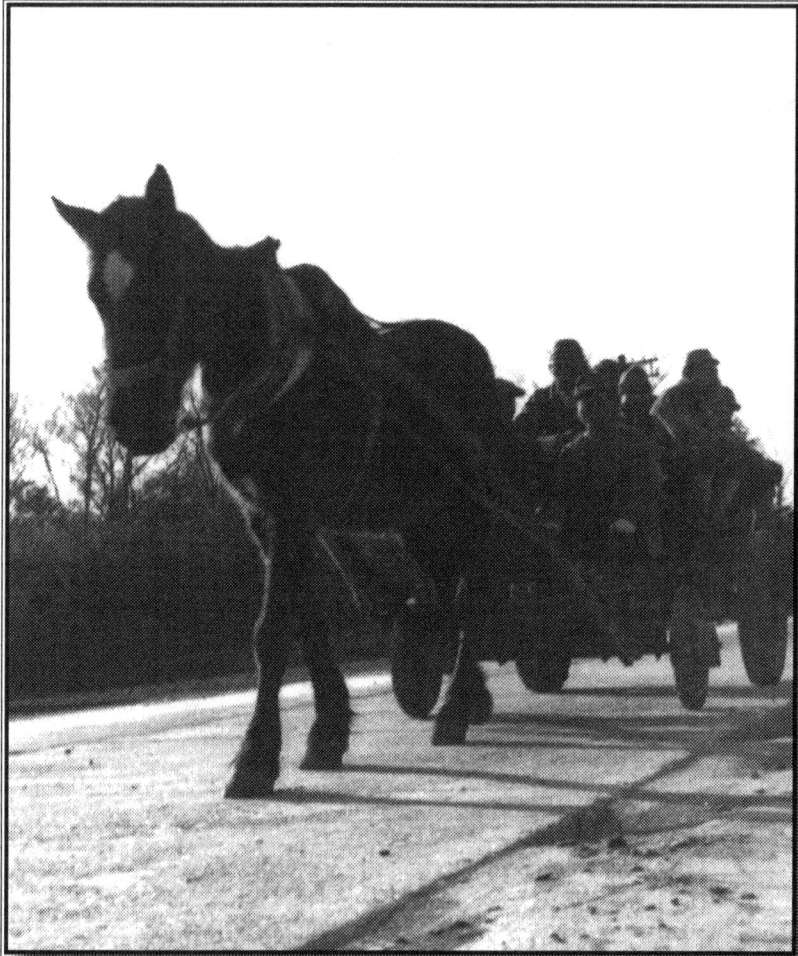

The Solid World Is Dissolving

In going or returning
they are pulled by a dray horse
along a rutted road to rice-fields
it is not day but just before it
or just at the end of it
light leaks out bright in promise
or extinction
the farmers glimpse
the foreigner by the side of the road
each a brief aside
in the life of the other
in the middle of the festival
of the rice seedlings
the sound of flutes and gongs
fill the air there is dancing
& singing there is this ritual
they are growing grain
for their children's children
an offering for their ancestors
who day by day
they are becoming

Walls

See the saffron light suffusing
The temple the distant triangular roof
High above the walls the hard-packed ground
What did it mean to you
This wholeness without suffering or
Resurrection just the patient indwelling
The waiting the clean movement
From one breath to the next
From day to night from emptiness to emptiness
From form to form as twilight closes in
In the rising darkness there is
The sense of no becoming
There is the loveliness of poise
The walls and trees are already shadows
Of what they always were

Reliquary

On a straw mat in a newly-harvested field
    an old woman in a faded black robe kneels
to pick through
    a small flower-patterned box
in her left hand she holds some folded bills
    with her right she picks among the leftovers of an older life
a porcelain saki cup a tin can a stack of knitted pot-holders
    arranging them here there
according to some half-recollected plan—
    of the legions of sharp-edged bamboo blades littered about her
each one leaps out urgent in its clarity
    as if the strewn-about bodies were a testament
to some unimaginable catastrophe
    and she the sole survivor
were fated to pick through them
    nothing less real than the world
these relics were a part of
    nothing more real than the loss of it
everything banished to being
    a souvenir among souvenirs
ribbons hanging out of a box

Vestigial

It's a still life of a Japanese farm
      & the thatch of the small farmhouse roof
and the tall leafy carefully cut trees overlooking it
      are so close they could be growing out of it
the yard is full of rickety wooden fences running riot
      it is unclear what is being fenced in or out
this is what it would be like after the next apocalypse
      nothing would be different nothing would be strange
except the strangeness that comes from there being
      nothing but the silence in which voices once contended
here everything is abandoned everything a sign
      of human use or human loss
like the black old-fashioned bicycle propped up against a smooth tree-trunk
      for generations its long thin shadow has been slanting against
the hard-packed earth
      in the distance there is a field wild with scraggly leafless trees
and wild branches growing crazy
      and beyond that
dark mountains and a sky growing blacker and blacker
      as if it mattered to those
who once knelt against the earth

Once

"And if two sisters were running into the late afternoon glare
The larger after the smaller
Their feet flying along the dusty road
Next to the rice field with workers
Then later they might remember
Themselves that way
Running for the sake of running
In a world still without dread"

From the Ship, a Coastline

"That would be waving and that would be crying
    crying and shouting and meaning farewell"
but there could be neither waving nor shouting
    even if everything was a way of saying farewell
without saying it farewell farewell farewell
    farewell in the eyes farewell in the hands
farewell in the words the inchoate half-legible words
    the rasped-out words
a different alphabet for a different world
    the words the pencil traced the torn words
words that could not be seen
    the torn words fluttering down
words of petition
    words I have only words
will you do this?
    death-words balm-words
the words in the eyes pleading
    words to carry on the first duty
the old duty
    heaven itself a way of crying and shouting
and meaning farewell

Notes

The photographs referenced in this book range from sepia images of the Pacific Ocean to images of a ravaged Tokyo and Japan's impoverished countryside in the aftermath of World War II. Rather than simply describing the photographs, the poems employ them as points of departure: they exist as a force field of historical memory, of imagined historical memories, of voices then and now, of voices recovered only in the re-imagination of them. The poems, that is, try to open up a dialogue between the various pasts of "then" and the various presents of "now." Haunted by the silences in those vivid, preternaturally sharp black-and-white images, the poems seek to make present those hauntings, and to make the present more answerable to all the pasts that make it up.

The Book of the Floating World is loosely based on the photographs of Occupied Japan around 1945 or early 1946 taken by the sculptor, William J. Thompson, then nineteen or so.

"Idolatry"

Kusunoki Masahige (?-1336) was a medieval warrior who became regarded by the Japanese as a great legendary hero for his loyalty to the emperor. Prior to World War II, young people in Japan were taught to dedicate their lives to the emperor just as Kusunoki did. A bronze statue of Kusunoki stands in front of the Imperial Palace in Tokyo. In 1336 Kusunoki decided to confront a powerful enemy at Minatogawa (near modern Kobe City), but he lost the battle and committed suicide.

"The Names"

The poem refers to General MacArthur's General Head Quarters, the site of power during the American Occupation. In theory, from there, MacArthur attempted to reorganize the Japanese government along the lines of American democracy.

"Blossoms"

The photograph is of Ueno Park, a famous public park in northern Tokyo.

"Empire"

The occasion for the poem is a photograph of the American Embassy in Tokyo; the last five sentences are from Koshino Ayako's recollection of the postwar period. C.f. Haruko Taya Cook and Theodore F. Cook, eds. *Japan at War* (New York: The New Press, 1992).

"At the Gate"

The poem refers to a *torii* gate. Torii are dramatic gates that stand at the entrances to Shinto shrines, marking the sacred ground beyond. It is believed that worshippers are purified as they pass through them. A torii has two round upright columns and two crossbeams.

"Body/Art"

This sequence is based on a series of intricate multicolor full-body tattoos (*irezumi*) of Japanese men, wearing only loincloths or *fundoshi*. These tattoos, made up of intertwined images, frequently include legendary figures and ordinary objects invested with mythological significance. The art of tattoos is an ancient one in Japan, with a rich tradition but it is now dying out.

Daruma, also known as Bodai Daruma, is the legendary religious teacher credited with having brought the Chan or Zen sect of Buddhism from India to China, where he was known as Bodhidharma in the sixth century A.D.

Nakama, meaning a set, a circle, a coterie, defines all those who are on the "inside," all the others being on the "outside." Any single Japanese belongs to many such nakama.

The cherry blossom in Japanese culture is frequently associated with all that is transient and evanescent in life.

The Japanese translation of the fourteenth-century Chinese novel *Shu-hu Chuan* (*Suikoden* in Japanese) became a craze in the early 1800s. *Suikoden* describes the exploits of Sung Chiang and his rebel companions during the first two decades of the twelfth century. Each section of the book tells of one man and his adventures, but all are bound together by the single theme of revolt against the corrupt bureaucracy. Forming a Robin-Hood-like band, they exhibited their humanity, their decency, and their sense of rightness.

Kuniyoshi produced a magnificent illustrated edition of Suikoden; his illustrations became immensely popular and formed both the style and iconography of the Japanese pictorial tattoo. See Donald Richie and Ian Buruma's *The Japanese Tattoo* (New York: Weatherhill, 1980).

"Self-Portrait"

Refers to a drawing William Thompson did of himself while in Japan.

"Honganji Temple"

Amida is an important figure in Mahayana Buddhism. Amida is believed to have made a great vow to help all suffering beings and when this was fulfilled, he immediately became a Buddha. His followers taught that anyone could be blissfully reborn by having faith in Amida and by repeating his name with a prayer known as the *nembutsu*. This tradition developed into "The Pure Land" sect of Buddhism; Honganji Temple is a key site for it.

"Honganji Temple II"

Echoes certain phrases of Li-Young Lee's "This Room and Everything in It."

"Asaka"

The location of the army base where William Thompson was stationed; at the time, it was a predominantly agricultural area.

"Mount Fuji"

Mount Fuji is the highest and most graceful mountain in Japan, and a world-famous symbol of the country. Since ancient times, male religious pilgrims have climbed it. A Shinto shrine to Konohana Sakyua Hime, a divine princess, is maintained on the summit.

"The Solid World Is Dissolving"

The title is a phrase from James Joyce's "The Dead."

"From the Ship, a Coastline"

"That would be waving and that would be crying/Crying and shouting and meaning farewell" are the first two lines of Wallace Stevens's poem "Waving Adieu, Adieu, Adieu."

Index of First Lines

About the Author

Jon Thompson is a professor of English at North Carolina State University, where he teaches courses in twentieth century literature. In addition to his publications in poetry, he has published *Fiction, Crime and Empire* (University of Illinois Press, 1993). He also edits *Free Verse: A Journal of Contemporary Poetry & Poetics* and is the editor of the Parlor Press's new poetry series, Free Verse Editions.